AF268435

Published in the United Kingdom in 2021 on behalf of MumWrite by streetcake magazine, 124 Cadogan Terrace, London, E9 5HP.

First printing, 2021

ISBN 978-1-8380960-3-8

Cover design by Nikki Dudley

Template design by Alec Newman

Edited by Nikki Dudley

Contents

Foreword

MumWrite began as a lockdown project that was a way in which to build a community, to write, and to provide a space where mums could create without feeling judged. We all know what it's like when you turn up to a workshop looking dishevelled, tired, and underprepared, worried that your kids will run in, don't we? Well, MumWrite has consistently countered this and given mums a place where they don't need to worry about any of those things!

This year, the community of mums has continued to grow, and it's been one of my favourite things watching the mums who have met through MumWrite forming their own relationships, supporting one another, and collaborating to do exciting projects or writing. I didn't realise how far-reaching MumWrite would be.

In this anthology, there's a mixture of writing from recent MumWriters and other mums who have impacted on the programme in one way or another - as advocates, as founding members, as guest writers, and as mums who are backbones of the mum writing community - who all deserve space to have their words celebrated.

MumWrite has moved to a paid-for model, but I try to keep it as affordable as possible because I want mums to be able to access it. What's been amazing is seeing mums pay extra for workshops in order for another mum to attend - it makes my heart warm everytime it happens. THIS is the spirit of MumWrite and something I hope continues.

I hope you enjoy the anthology, and thank you for your support. You are part of the MumWrite community as much as the participants.

Nikki Dudley

MumWrite facilitator

a Boy Worth Having won't take no for an answer; he'll woo me, buy me flowers, take me on dinner dates. Wait. 'This is very important,' she says. 'You need to make him feel like he's won a prize.'

When a Boy Worth Having asks me to dance, I follow Mother's advice, say no. Think he'll ask again. Instead, he asks Meredith. They gyrate under glitter-hot lights and after, she spreads her legs. Three months later they're married.

'Only because they had to,' Mother says.

Other Boys Worth Having ask me, but I keep saying no, until they stop. I can't forget that first one, the one I really wanted, the one who now has two more babies with Meredith – my sister, Meredith, whose motto in life has always been: Fuck what Mother says.

The sleep myth

sleep

   the most

underestimated treasure

can't accumulate it

    hard to find

and the saying:

   sleep like a baby

let me tell you

it's a myth

<u>**Support**</u>

Support bra,

Baby bump support belts,

Antenatal support,

Support your perineum,

Supportive relatives,

Is support needed?

A&E Emergency Support,

PND support,

Breastfeeding support,

Mastitis support,

Support those separated stomach

muscles,

ALWAYS

SUPPORT THE

BABY'S HEAD,

Recovery support,

Support your children,

Support yourself,

CBT support,

Support your husband,

Support your friends,

Support on the bus,

Support in the shop,

Support with carrying the

buggy downstairs,

I can't do it support,

Crying in pjs support,

Hiding in the kitchen drinking

coffee and eating chocolate

support,

A tiny text from you support,

Thank you support,

You can do it support,

You got this support.

<u>Whatever you need is OK</u>

<u>support.</u>

This circle

My back-body springs alive, made of fire,
knitted in sinew, clustered

under woollen blankets.
Tiny fingers cascade

on nipples pink and rough,
as a baby animals tongue.

Abandoned light clusters
in windpipes and veins,

filling gaps
left by forgotten meals.

It leaks ultraviolet
while I ooze goo

white and sweet
this dispersal is my solitary task.

I am vessel lessening,
and endlessly
replenishing.

ANDA   PARA   ANDA

                   WALK   STOP   WALK

PARA   ANDA   PARA   ANDA   PARA   ANDA

                   STOP   WALK   STOP

ANDA   PARA   ANDA   PARA   ANDA   PARA

                   WALK   STOP   WALK

                               ANDA   PARA   ANDA

                   WALK   STOP   WALK

ANDA   PARA   ANDA

                   STOP   WALK   STOP

PARA   ANDA   PARA

                   WALK   STOP   WALK

ANDA   PARA   ANDA

Mother Star & Daughter

<u>Mother Star</u>

I wish upon the stars
that hold my mother's soul
wish
that I can pluck it from the night
and hold it.

The stars twinkle back
custodians
remind me
I already have her soul.
Daughter.

<u>Daughter</u>

of moon and dust
I see you.

Soft in shadows,
hard in the spotlight,
you tend to each new day
even though,

even
though.

This is a call and response between writing buddies: 'Mother Star' by Emma Jones, 'Daughter' by Marcelle Newbold

Cycling and galleries on love's latest data dump

"To appear rich, we become poor." - Marguerite Blessington, an Irish novelist

It was half past four and me coming out of nowhere meanwhile
I believe in the ever healing power of unconditional blue love, sure
I wish everyday was a state exam, I told her, rules *are* friends.
Indeed!
"What does an autopsy smell like?" Asked his twin brother, the
poor créatúr, sure he'd only ever been only known in death now.

Why are there so many   g _ p s   in my   h e _ r t ?

I was told to ask a god for answers once. We met one late
afternoon, me and god decided to finally use the good fleece
blankets to sit on the couch to watch 'Love Island 2018' both
ignoring the cold cactuses rolling outside the window, and I even
gave her a sun hat for the walk home through the Great Sand Dune
Storms, let's leave the begging of oil on canvas or melting marble
for another time.

She stops. Pulls shoe from under bed,
"Unconditional love, that you?"

Laughs. Laughs again, prephas a little too wildly. Should we send someone in?

- One blink - one.
- Two blinks - yes.

Don't stay for the kids

I took my diamond ring off.
It now lies a drawer.
White gold size L.
It gave me a rash,
an itch so constant that the only remedy was to remove it.
To remove myself.

Now I have a diamond tattooed behind my ear.
I got it on a second date,
giddy with possibilities.
We kissed at the bus stop but I already knew he wasn't for me.

An old lady told me it would feel like kisses on my neck.
I cursed her.
The sound of the needle buzzing.
Ink scraping into bone.
No flesh to cushion the pain.

A permanent symbol of
my strength
or
how
much
shit
one person stays for.
Long overdue.
I was a person I no longer liked.
He was a person who no longer liked me.

Do not stay for the kids.

What I didn't think about

I ate copious jelly babies
       the day
       you were born

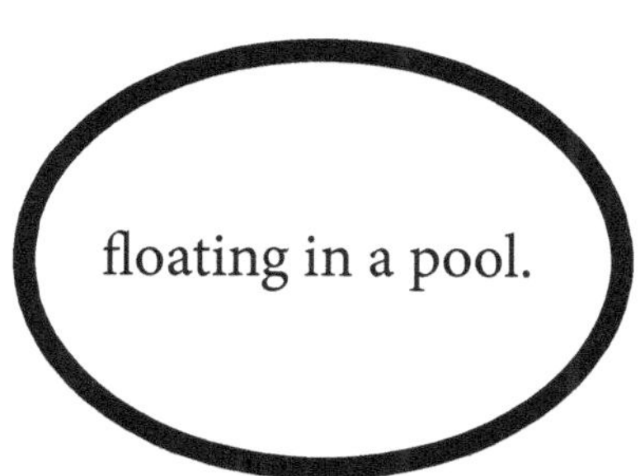

But not
the red ones

       [I hate the red ones]

The midwives took bets, counting ::::minutes::::
me-count-ing-every-second-waiting-for
             searing
             red
             burst
             (translation: your arrival).

White sheets saturated with redness when
they threw a crying red lump at me.

                That
                    moment
                       waiting
for a breath, ignoring
the red
       removed   from   me –
       ~~never mine again.~~

Suturing raw skin / blood smeared gloves /
empty words overflowing
              what did you say?
            what did you say?

Just a tear echoing in the brain – the sound of

'no way back'

Clenched fists and tried not to think about

blood building, the crime scene on the bed

swept away as if I hadn't
            bled myself out.

                BUT THE EVENT IS
            RECORDED IN MY BODY,
            THE WAY NEW SKIN GROWS
                AND --FUSES--
            BONES RE-MOLDED,
            FORENSIC EVIDENCE IS
                MY VERY INSIDES

a puzzle
            never
                quite
                                    fitting.

Later, in the night-time, balancing
in the bathroom, as if on a pencil,
        a dark red fleshy mass
        falls out
        like an asteroid casually hitting the floor.

There's no one else and I
tried not to think about ███
The red alarm button winked at me like an exit lane

MumWrite

and   I called out.

"Don't worry," they said.   "Look after that baby." "Just get some sleep."

Scooping cold Weetabix with milk and sugar
        / into my mouth / holding you /
        making me feel
        alive and trying not to
        think about blood.

                How it pulsed out / seeped out /
                        pooled around / me /
                        grieving the body
                and you wonder (how much is left in there?)

I drank tea and watched you breathing, **in and out**, in and
tried not to
[most definitely didn't]
think about ▮▮▮ and that line

        between what is
                inside the body and
                                what is not.

In the bathroom, in the eerie quiet
of the birth ward, the lights off
to not wake you,   the red light
                                            was the end
                                            of your dock,
                                            I reached out but
                                            you slept indifferently
                                            and I promise

I didn't [not for a moment]
think about   death.

The narcissist's mirror

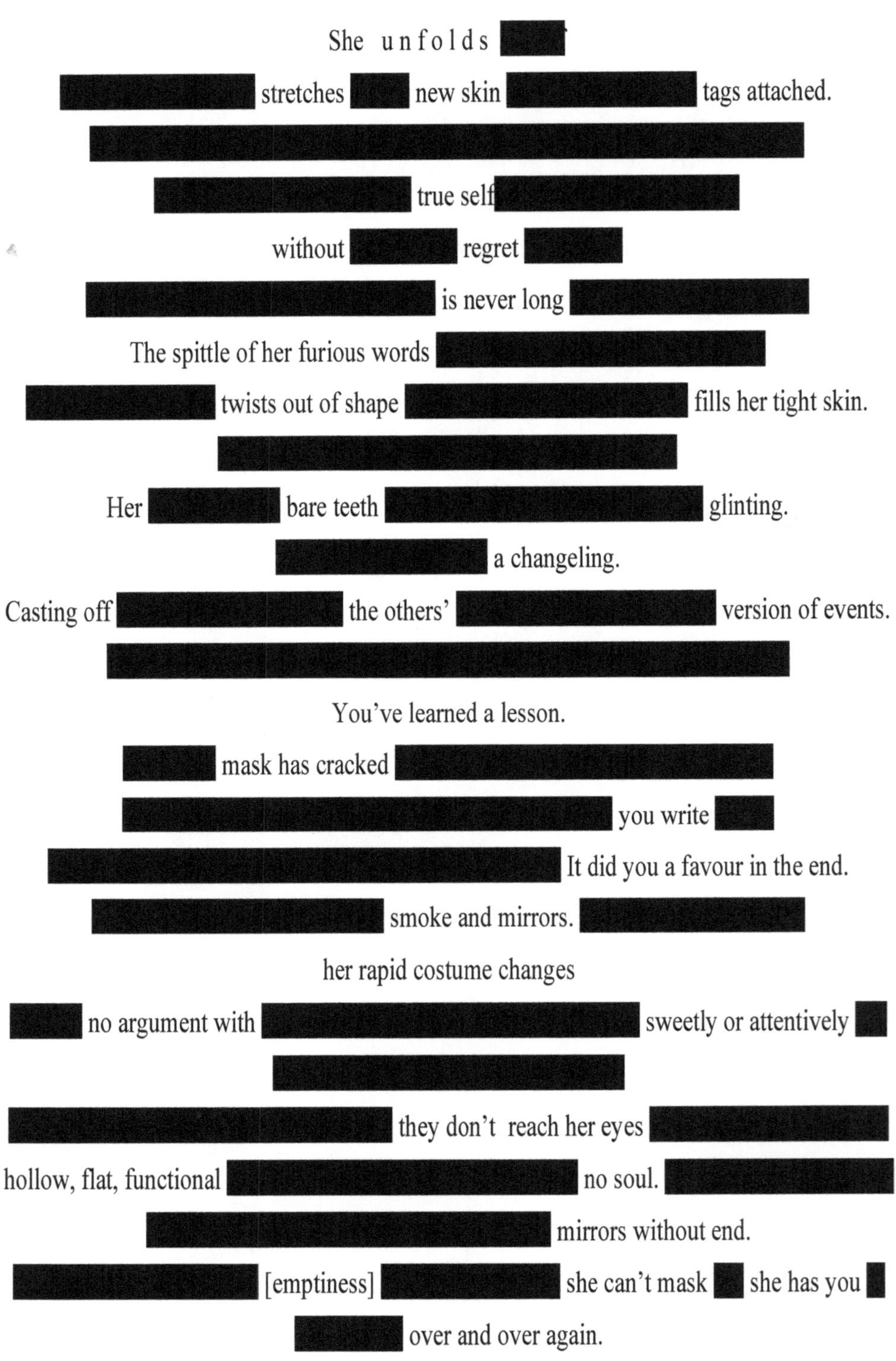

MumWrite

Entrances and exits

There's a new way into me
ever since you came along.
I feel it monthly, when the
scaffold buckles beneath the
rest of me. When my legs pull
away, at my hips. At the seams.

shift / right / sway / shift / left / sway / shift

I feel it when I swim, breaststroke
just as I was taught. Strong armed,
frog-legged, always keep your head
above the water. Trying to get a handle
on what's left of this body, this back.

water in / water out / water in / water out / water

You cleared the path with your size, and
sheer determination, and a little help, a
pair of latex hands and metal rods. Now
Daddy doesn't hurt anymore. Doesn't feel
like very much anymore. But we still try our
best. At night, or whenever you're asleep.

thrust / pull / clench / thrust / pull / clench

Mother and Child Reunion

We are having a baby.

We have decided.

It has taken nine months of discussion, indecision, planning and saving. I am excited and scared in equal measure. My wife is delighted and doubtful. She had always assumed, since this is what I told her, that I did not want to have children. I had accustomed myself to the fact that it wouldn't happen. That I wouldn't meet the right woman, or I wasn't in the "right place", being neither financially solvent, nor mentally stable.

I told her this, six months after we met, to give her a chance to call it off before things got too serious. I told her on her birthday, at a restaurant in Paris. It was perhaps not the best moment, but she handled the news pretty well in the circumstances. For three years or so, remaining childless was a choice, that became a fact, that we did not question again.

Until now.

We might have remained content with this decision if it wasn't for her mother dying. No one expected this to happen so soon. It upended our life as much as it ended hers. My wife became her mother's carer: she fed her, washed her and dressed her, when she could still get out of bed. As she sunk further and further into endless hospital pillows, she held her mother's hand and read to her. When that became too much, all any of us could do was smile encouragingly, and touch her gently, her fingers flittering in our palms like tiny butterflies.

A small dancing flicker of hope, that we were careful not to crush.

During the unexpected yet inevitably quick decline and death of her mother, my wife (then girlfriend) became the de facto parent, not just for her mother but for her father too: making arrangements, decisions, rotas and tea. Actually, I made the tea, that was all I could usefully offer my family-in-law to-be.

And after all the flowers and cards, the curtains remaining closed in the daytime, the constant phone calls of condolences, subdued neighbours and unannounced visits from unknown

 MumWrite

work colleagues, after all that: nothing. A great yawning chasm of nothing. No proper goodbyes, no parting words, no final kiss. Just this: an aching tear ripping my wife apart, and tears of grief for a mother lost far too soon and far too young.

My wife became her grief. She wore it like a dark cloak hiding herself from the world, shrouding herself in darkness as summer drew near. But she needed that grief, something to cling onto, to replace the piercing loss inside. And although the days eventually grew brighter and life went on in the way that it does, things had changed, something had shifted, and we would never be the same again.

My wife often cried at night during this period. She slept foetal position, and sometimes I couldn't wake her from her haunted dreams. She took to sleeping with an old ragdoll she'd had as a child, rescued from her parents' house whilst caring for her mother. She slept with it tucked close to her chest, protecting it, stroking it, needing it as a mother needs her child. We hadn't spoken about "it", we hadn't needed to. It was obvious how much she wanted to have a child, how becoming a mother herself would somehow replace the loss of her own mother. A way to feel close to her again.

We didn't talk about having a baby in quite those terms, it was too close to a truth too painful to admit. But one night the topic came up, and I didn't brush it aside as I might have done before. I said maybe we could think about it, maybe we could start planning, and then maybe we could just…see what happens. She wept. Tears of joy and sorrow. Of grief and relief.

We are fortunate that what used to be termed natural conception is now frowned upon, even banned in some parts of the country, since the risks of mutation or chemically-induced deformities are too great. Now that most couples opt for what's known as planned pregnancy, we are able to take advantage of this too, since as two women we are entirely lacking in sperm. We can build our baby from scratch.

We opt for the standard insertion and extraction process, but can now afford (thanks to my mother in law's will) to choose the genetic material for fertilisation. Now that it's possible to use DNA from the stem cells of another person, male or female, we are able to have a child that is biologically both of ours.

It was always going to be a girl. On that we were both adamant. Bringing up a girl means there is less chance of passing on the genetic deformities that have been discovered in the sperm of most men over the last 30 years. Aside from doing our bit for the preservation of humanity, it feels easier to bring another female into our midst. No boy bits to worry about.

Then I had the idea.

It was an obvious solution, but I had to act quickly. I made the necessary preparations, which was easier than expected, since everyone's genetic template is registered. From the various hospital procedures my wife's mother had gone through in their attempts to save her, there was enough genetic material to create a good DNA sample. Then it was simply a question of switching the samples. From mine to hers.

After so many years of wanting, my wife will finally have the chance to be a mother. To not only have a baby, but to mother her own mother. To have her and hold her again. A chance also, for her mother to live again; to be reborn, literally. And for us to care for her and love her and ensure that no harm should come to her. It is a second chance; things will be different this time.

My wife will be reunited with her mother: adoring, newborn and vulnerable, holding onto her daughter's hand as she did in her last moments.

We are having a baby.

I have decided.

The extraction is next week. I can't imagine how women

coped with this in the old days, going through such a painful and risky labour. So much better for child and mother to have it done through a planned surgical procedure.

I won't tell my wife about the switch I made to the DNA sample just yet. Maybe not for the first few months. I shall tell her later once we've settled into a routine of sorts. Once mother and child have bonded. And reunited.

I can't wait to see the look on her face.

Beauty's sister

It quivers into a whisper -
U s e l e s s.
The words ring out
    I. am. Paralysed.
My name?
Beauty's Sister.

Elasticity? No longer.
(The result of my tension.)
Lines like violet ribbons
Drape the sandy dune.
They are all I have.

I am pressed against
A broken window,
Wishing, with all my heart
I was strong.

My tears close the tomb
Seal it with lilies.

The dust gathers
My self, s
          i
            n
              k
                i
                  n
                    g.

Beauty's Sister
The dry river.

                                                            Crushed.

The words
Keep coming
Back / the words.
I am drowning in them.
U s e l e s s.

I am divided every few months
After flowering.
Beauty's sister or roguish matron?
Either way,
They blew out the candle.

The dune is swept away
But the ribbons remain.

I look to the cuckoo
Her world expands
And unlocks.
The snow gathers - but her nest is warm.
She is delivered / reviled.

Beauty's Sister?
No.
Sister's Beauty.
I am the cuckoo.

I am strong.

#TheyCutWeBleed

Universal credit & child tax credit, two's your limit.
The Iron Lady's second coming, pushing young
professionals with five figures owing into parents' homes,
into youth cocaine comas. Doing fucking nothing
for females on the front line. The yes women,
the rosette wearers, social media sharers, photo op posers,
teams turn the hungry migrants away, we're full
to the brim and the NHS is on its knees.

Take a seat and wait to be seen.

And I touch my body

And I touch my body, like a boy I remember

all invisible finger tips
slow curve trace -
my forearm, a nape.

The kettle boils

and space closes -
so I roll down my sleeves,
dinner plates now clean,

and return to company, with coffee.

Acknowledgements

A big thanks to Alec Newman, who helped with the typesetting and design. Thanks for making this look good!

Thanks to Joe Ruddock for supporting me and encouraging me with MumWrite, especially in the evenings and weekends to deliver workshops and make the best of the programme. Thanks to my kids for thinking that mum writes all the poems in the world!

Thanks to all who have shared the programme and the MumWriters for joining in MumWrite with me! Thanks to Anna Caig and Laura Besley for making guest appearances.

Thanks to anyone who has supported another mum to attend a workshop and acted as someone else's cheerleader.

I would like to also acknowlege that my poem, 'What I didn't think about' was first published in *-algia* zine.

Useful resources for mums

#PNDHour is a Twitter chat every Wednesday 8-9pm for
maternal mental health peer support run via
@PNDandMe

The Breastfeeding Network - breastfeedingnetwork.org.uk

Mothers who Make - motherswhomake.org

Parents 1st - parents1st.org.uk

PANDAs Foundation - pandasfoundation.org.uk

The Letters of Light Project - lettersoflightproject.com

Birth Trauma Association - birthtraumaassociation.org.uk

The Mum Poem Press - themumpoempress.com

WriteClub - writeclub.org.uk